Copyright © 2024 by Hawa Who

Edition: April 2025
ISBN: 979-8-89901-161-0

Published by Primedia eLaunch LLC

THE CONTENT

CHAPTER 01: THE FIRST HEARTBEAT

I wasn't looking.

You weren't either.

But there you were—

a vibe I didn't expect.

Not love,

just a spark,

one heartbeat.

The kind that makes you pause,

but you pretend you didn't feel it.

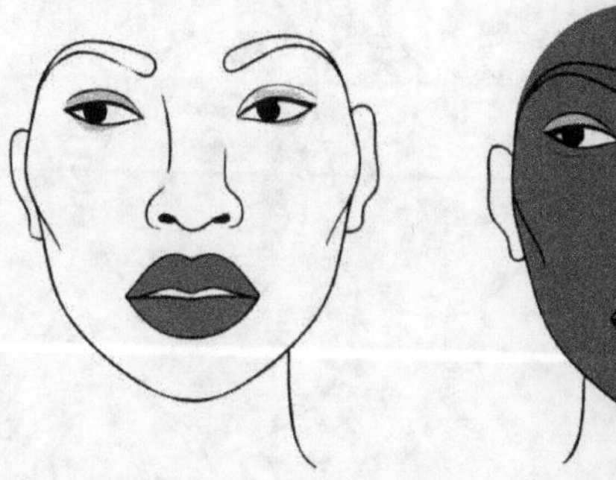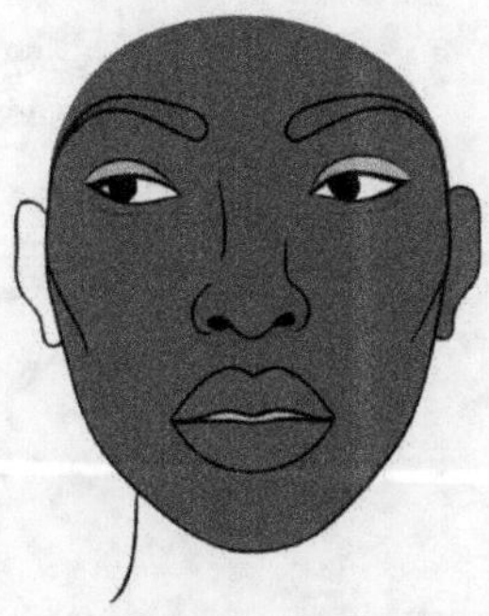

I told myself it was nothing

But you knew, didn't you?

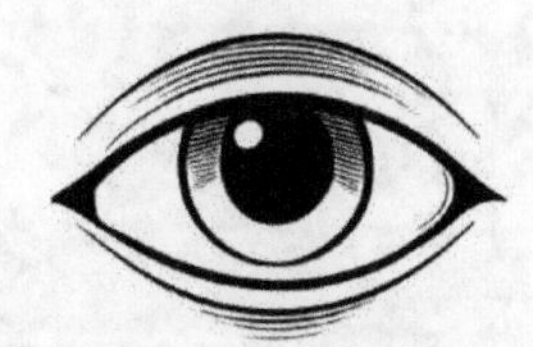

We lock eyes—

I look away.

Why am I running?

I wasn't ready to be seen

the way you saw me.

You found me—

unfiltered,

unguarded.

The parts I hide

were already yours.

Suddenly,

it's not just my world anymore.

You're not love—yet.

But you're something

And that's enough

to make me want more.

So, do I chase it?

Do I run?

Either way,

you caught me.

CHAPTER 02: UNHINGED

I don't know where I am

or

Who's driving the effing car

Relationships,

Your Brain gets used to it.

But your heart never does.

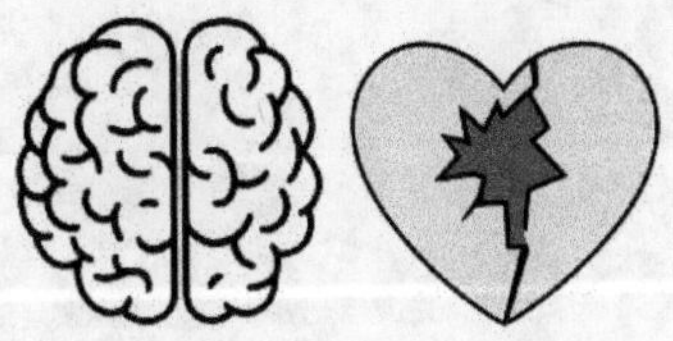

I've always had control.

Over my thoughts.
Over my body.
Over my heart.

It's what kept me safe,
what kept me **ME**.

But you?

You didn't just
walk in—you *unraveled* me.
Piece by piece, without even trying.
I didn't see it coming,
wasn't even looking,
but there you were—
A beautiful regret in my head. Yet in my heart a
soothing cave.

You can stay

I LOVE YOU

Do you think of me?
I find myself asking,
even when I know it's ridiculous,
even when I tell myself to let it go.

We've gotten too close

if you left, I would still find you.

Do you think of me?
Or am I just another moment in your chaos?
You have this way of making me feel alive,
yet lost,
as if I'm grasping at shadows,
trying to piece together a reality

that feels more like a dream.

And here I am,

caught in this delusion,
twisting my own thoughts into knots,
because *how could someone like you
ever think of someone like me?*

27

I'm spiraling,

trying to hold onto
sanity

while you're this beautiful enigma,
a whirlwind of uncertainty.
You say I'm special,
but then there are those moments—
the silence, the distance—
that makes me feel like

I'm not even a blip on your radar.

Do you think of me?

am I just a figment of my imagination,
crafted by the way you look at me
and then look away?
I'm gaslit and dizzy,
caught in this cycle of wanting more
while knowing I shouldn't.

And now, here I am, caught between wanting to scream
and laugh, lost in this chaos you've created, yet somehow
still craving more of it. Because even in the madness,
you make me feel alive.

I look in the mirror,
and I don't recognize the reflection staring back—
just a girl lost in a labyrinth of confusion,
her heart racing for someone who barely glances
back.
Every moment spent waiting,
every question left unanswered,
weighs heavy on my chest,
like a stone that's sinking deeper.

This isn't love;

it's haunting,

a ghost that lingers,
and I'm left chasing phantoms,
clutching at memories of what could've been,
while losing sight of who I am.

We both know we buried our dreams.
What we had was never built to last.

You're painting me the wrong color—

it's not red, it's green.
It's not me its **YOU**.

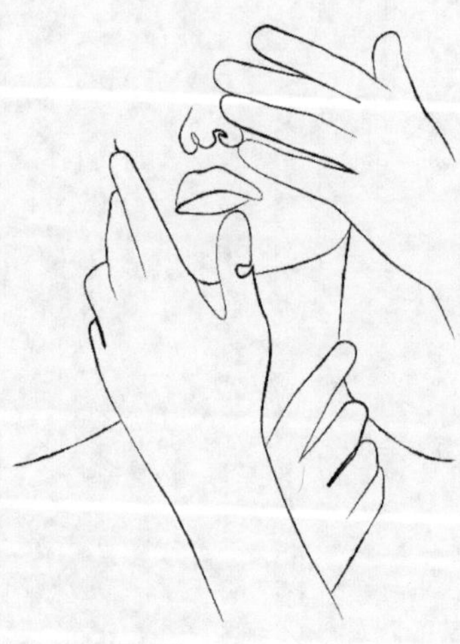

I LOST ME

in looking for you

Craving your presence yet drowning in my absence.
And in this whirlwind of emotions,

I pause.
I realize—
I've become so consumed by the chase
that I've lost the very essence of me.

CHAPTER 03: CAUGHT ME AT THE RIGHT TIME

Hawa Who – You're A Lover Girl

She Just Wanted to be loved

Maybe love was never hers

His skin attached to hers

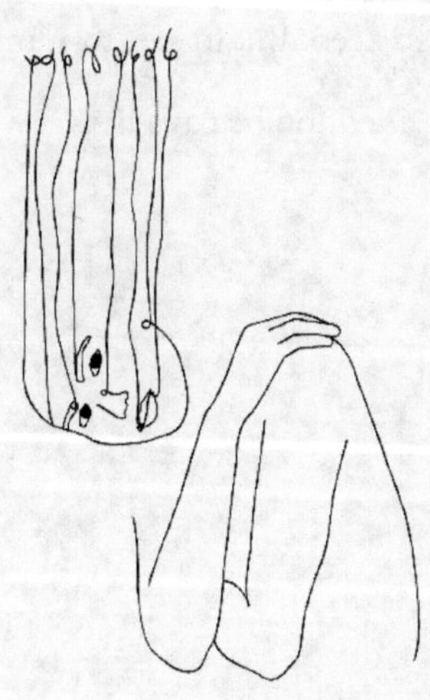

She Caved then she became his

Not to keep. But to see, to admire.

She loves the attention he gave her.

It was the right time.

It was her time.

He felt it was his time

A battle.

Please swing my way

What am I to do when in need of your love.

YOU SAID YOU WANTED LOVE!

When I was in shambles

You ate me up

Honey save it for the old me!

45

Give me LOVE

Stop with WORDS

I thought I locked away my past,
but it lingers,
like that playlist I can't delete,
the one that hits too close to home.

Routines, Routines, Routines
I never nailed the goodbye,
especially the ones I never saw coming.

His voice memo from 33 weeks ago

IT GOES.

"I JUST GOT BACK HOME

PLEASE CALL ME BACK MY LOVE"

TRUST THAT I DID CALL HIM BACK.

HE CAUGHT ME,

AND IT WAS THE RIGHT TIME!

In every laugh, I hid my tears,
brushed it off like it was no big deal.
But you're here now,
and everything feels raw.

Can you see the real me?
The girl who just wants a moment,
a little love,

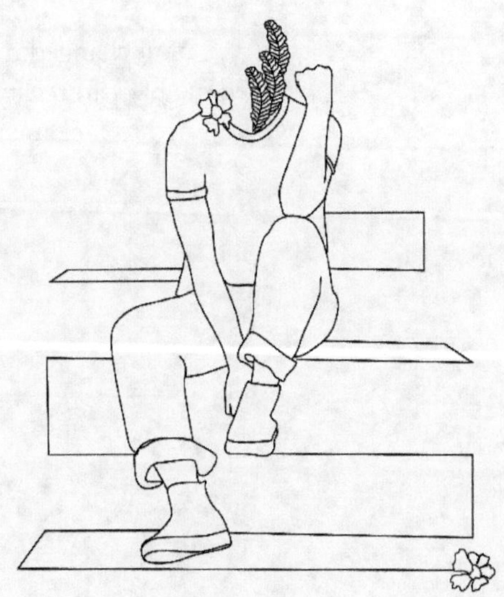

like the kind I never knew.

You changed me,
pulled me back to reality,
where I had to face my truths.

I wonder if you realize
how you flip my world,
like a favorite song that keeps coming back
but never gets old.

I've carried this load for so long,
heavy yet light,
like I'm floating when you're around.

You're not just a fling,
you set the mood,
reminding me what it's like
when love doesn't sting.

But here I am,
torn between wanting to hold you close
and freaking out about the plunge,
the deep end of love that could swallow
me whole.

What if I lose myself again,
caught up in the whirlwind of us?
The highs that feel like euphoria
and the lows that hit like a brick.

But maybe,
just maybe,
this time it's okay to jump,
to let you take the lead
and trust the fall.

So here we stand,
you and me,
caught in this messy dance,
but it feels so damn right.
Maybe it's time to ride the wave
and see where it takes us.

CHAPTER 04:

LOVE BOMBED

Love Bombed
Let's get into it—

a story of how I never saw it coming.
This is my story.

He seized my heart with sweet

whispers and tender promises,
Held it like it meant something
Then he wrecked it—
Fed it to the wolves and walked away like it was
nothing.

But little did he know,
The WOLVES saw the value of my heart,
So they gave it back.

Love Bombing

Love bombing is when someone sweeps into your life and creates a sweet, romantic image of themselves, carefully crafted to win your heart. They shower you with affection, sweet words, and grand gestures, making you feel special. But it's all a façade—a calculated plan with no intention of keeping their promises.

Over time, their charm fades because it was never real. They weren't genuinely interested in building something meaningful; they just wanted to claim you. Their goal wasn't love—it was possession. They saw you, admired everything you are, and decided they *had* to have you.

So, they orchestrated this performance of love. And it worked. You fell for it. You got love bombed.

The difference between love bombing and genuine interest lies in consistency. A person who is truly invested in you won't stop showing up once they've "gotten" you. But a love bomber will. Slowly, they become inconsistent, withdrawing the affection and kindness they used to hook you.

What remains is their true self—one that never intended to meet your emotional needs.

So yeah, here I am.
Love bombed.

I didn't see it coming—
how could I?
When the beginning was magic,
a flood of warmth that promised safety,
a whirlwind of whispered words
that wrapped around me like a soft lullaby.

"You're everything I've ever wanted."
"You're my forever."

I held those words like sacred vows,
let them echo in my quiet moments,
let them rewrite the parts of me
that had forgotten how to hope.

But hope was the bait, wasn't it?
And I, the fool who bit too hard.

Suddenly, his eyes stopped

softening when they met mine.
His voice, once my refuge,
grew sharp,
indifferent.

And there I was,
grasping for pieces of a story
I thought we were writing together.

Love bombed.
Wrecked.

Now I'm left here,
scraping the ashes of something
that never really burned as bright
as I believed.

CHAPTER 05:

ME OR HER

THE OPENING

She's extremely beautiful

I cannot deny

Her beauty isn't my worry

I just wanted to be chosen

a lover girl too loyal for my own good.

Or maybe just a pick-me,

standing on the edge of his indecision,

a lover girl too loyal for my own good.

THE COMPETITION

Was it her laughter,
The way it filled a room and outshined mine?

Was it her eyes,
Or the way she never looked at him like I did—
With so much need?

Was it her freedom,
The way she didn't care to stay?
Because I stayed.
I always stayed.

A LOVER'S DOUBT

The guy that did me dirty still looks amazing.

HER SHADOW

Her silhouette eats.
He can have her.
It just kills me inside.
It's all in my insecurities—
She's a sweet girl.

THE WAITING GAME

He's hot and cold with his affection,
But at least I feel *loved*—
SOMETIMES.

ME AND HER

Caught in His Confusion

He never knew what he wanted.
He wanted the idea of both of us.

We both shined bright,
but we were different.
She was more lenient,
I was more upfront, assertive.

He loved her—

I lover her
and it's okay.
But when he left,
he emptied our light.

Me and her,
left to wonder,
left to feel as if we were the problem.

HIS BRAIN WAS MADE OF RICE

Here's where I go off—
let it all out,
but it's not who I am.

He lacked what he sought externally,
but never found it at home.

All is forgiven—
but that doesn't mean I forget.

Side Note:
I like to insult people just enough
so it doesn't really hurt THEM,
because it'll still make them laugh,
while I get my hurt out.

Hence why I say "His brain was made of rice"

I hope I made you giggle

xoxo, **HAWA WHO**

THE FINAL ACT

He never knew what he wanted.
But he knew what he was doing.
He played us both—
Toyed with hearts like they were strings to pull.
At the end of the day,
We were never more than a choice.
Not the right one, but the easy one.
And maybe that's what broke me the most—
The feeling of allowing him to make me feel

that I was never enough.

HER AND I

You know me—a lover girl.
She was just like me—
A girl searching for love where it couldn't be
found.
But she was different in ways I couldn't explain—
She never stayed when the love ran dry.
She left when the pain started showing,
And I...
I never stayed.
Not when my heart begged for peace.
Not when his absence became the loudest silence.

Her and I—we clocked the truth.
He wanted us to need him.
I wanted to tell her the truth—
I liked her more than I let on.
The truth is, we had mutual friends,
And I stayed so long because the "love" helped
me pass the time.
But now I know better.
The truth was never simple,
And I knew that if I stayed,
I'd just be another string in his tangled mess.

We both deserved love—
Just not from him.

TO GIVE LOVE YOU MUST KNOW LOVE

TO GIVE LOVE, YOU MUST KNOW LOVE. IT'S NOT JUST ABOUT LOVING SOMEONE ELSE, BUT LOVING YOURSELF FIRST. UNDERSTANDING YOUR WORTH, EMBRACING YOUR FLAWS, AND REALIZING THAT NO ONE CAN DEFINE YOUR LOVE BUT YOU.

THE RAW TRUTH

I'm feeling cunt.
It's not a term of hate,
But one of power—
A reminder that I'm ONE (HAWA a
lover girl).

I'm whole within.
I let this play too long,
Which in turn ate me up.
Boys can be gross,
But we love men.
He's only a boy if he doesn't see a
woman's value.
A man knows how to treat a woman.

Men PROTECT women, they DO NOT contribute to
what WOMEN need to be protected from!

Time has passed,
And pain has turned into memory.

.

CHAPTER 06:

PRINCESS TREATMENTS

Glitter and body oil,
Window shopping,

he's on FaceTime
He loves my Ayra Starr
mini skirt.

"Babe, your manicure is booked for 4 p.m."

I smile, glancing at my phone.

His message feels like the perfect start to my day—planned and thoughtful.

"K, I love you. Can you scoop me up?

I wanna be a passenger princess today,"

He replies, his voice like a soft, warm melody through the speaker.

It's almost as if he knows exactly what I need before I even say a word.

I laugh, a little amused. "Okay, see you soon."

It's not even a question anymore.

This is just how things go.

I've gotten used to this level of care,

the little things that make a self-care day feel more like a luxurious escape.

I love how he treats me—

always looking out for me,

making sure everything is perfect. It's routine, yet it never gets old.

The Princess Treatment: A Self-Care Day

Today's self-care day has been on my calendar for weeks.

It's my escape—my time to unwind, recharge,

and indulge in a little pampering.

Shopping, nails, reading, writing...

It's all about me today.

He knows how important this day is for me, and of course, he's all in. The plan is simple: he's driving me around, making sure I don't have to worry about a single thing. I get in the car, throw my things in the backseat, and instantly feel at peace. There's no rush, no pressure—just a day designed for me to enjoy the things I love.

As we pull out of the driveway, I put on my favorite playlist. I know the drill by now. He's the driver, I'm the passenger princess. And honestly? It feels *good*. Not because I'm being treated like royalty—though that's nice too—but because it's the kind of comfort that only comes from being understood. He gets it. He knows what I need without having to ask.

Xoxo   - **HE'S HIM**

I'm in his front seat,
The world outside fading into a blur.
The scent of his cologne lingers in the
air—
Soft, comforting,
Like home.
I sink into the seat,
A sigh escaping my lips,
And the day begins.

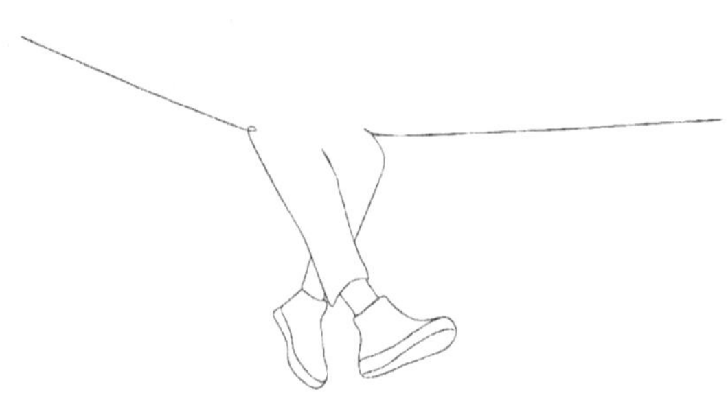

We roll through the streets,
The sun casting a golden hue over everything,
I'm taking selfies,
He gets it.
He almost expects it.
The way the light catches my face,
The perfect angle,
The smile I didn't have to force.
It's just us,
And the world seems to pause,
Like everything is exactly where it's supposed to
be.

He glances over,
A smirk tugging at his lips,
Knowing exactly what I'm doing.
The phone clicks,
The moment captured,
And I don't have to say a word—
He's already swiping through to see it.
"I look good," he says,
Grinning,
As if he's always known.

We share a laugh,
And I turn my attention back to the streets,
But the light feels warmer now,
More alive,
Because it's him and me,
Chasing the sunset in a world that's just ours.

I'm obsessed with him,
A king.

The way his hands grip
the wheel,
Eyes sharp, scanning the
road—
Protective, calculated,
Like he's the only one
who matters.

HE CARES FOR HIMSELF.

HE CARES FOR HUMANITY.

Ugh, my king.

He's so smart, a leader
So effortlessly funny,
Loves freely,
Without hesitation, without fear.

Human, raw, and real,
His love humane,
Like it's meant to be given
In its purest form.

He loves luxury—
Not for the label,
But for the craftsmanship,
The details that make something whole.
What can't he do?

A humanitarian,
A heart that reaches beyond his own.
He sees people,
Sees potential, sees hope.

He uses his goodness, he leads with goodness

I want to call him a fashion guy,
But that's not the label he wears.
He doesn't just dress,
He owns the room,
Owns the fabric, the thread,
Every inch of space he steps into.

Am I obsessed?
I am.
Cause he's him—
And there's nothing more real than that.

As the car hums along, I glance over at him again. There's something about the way he holds the wheel, steady and sure, like the world is his to command. But more than that, it's how he makes me feel—protected, seen, loved, and cherished. It's in the way he listens, even when it's just to the sound of my laughter. It's in how he notices the little things, like the small curl in my hair that I didn't even know was there.

But today, something else settles within me. As we cruise through the city, the world outside seems to blur and fade. For once, it's not just about the care and affection, the attention to detail, the luxury—it's about *me* too. In all this love, I realize something important.
I've been so caught up in the idea of being loved, of being treated like a queen, that I forgot what it means to be whole on my own. To *care* for myself with the same intensity that he cares for me. To feel like enough, without needing anyone to define my worth.

I smile quietly to myself. This self-care day, this *luxury*, isn't just about the manicures or the shopping sprees. It's about giving myself the same tenderness that he gives me. About realizing that I am my own person, with or without his love.
I look out the window, watching the world go by. There's a comfort in this, too. A peace in knowing that *I* am enough.

CHAPTER 07:

THE ONES WHO DON'T LIKE TO BE TOUCHED

There are some people who walk through this world with a quiet balance. They're not too loud, not too soft. They don't try to change the world, but somehow, the world can't help but change around them. And when you mess with them—when you try to make them bend to your will, your expectations, or your idea of who they should be—*you're doomed.*

I've learned this lesson more than once. At times, men who were interested in me came into my life, drawn to my presence, but not willing to understand the full depth of who I was. And I gave them a chance. I let them in, hoping they would see the person I am, the woman I carry inside of me. But instead of meeting me where I stood, they tried to shape me, mold me into something that would make sense in their world, something they could control.

They thought they could touch me in the ways that made sense to them. But they never asked how I wanted to be touched. They didn't try to learn my boundaries, my needs, or the rhythm of my heart. They only touched me with their own hands, trying to leave their mark, without realizing they were disrupting a balance that was already perfect.

The Dance of Touch

They touched me. Oh, how they touched me—hands on my skin, arms around me, lips pressed against mine. But they never truly *saw* me. They never understood the language of my touch, the way I wanted to be held, how my heart beat in sync with the rhythm of a deep connection, not a shallow one. I needed someone who could hear me when I said nothing, feel me when I was still. But instead, they tried to shape me to their needs, and in doing so, they lost me.

THEY GAVE ME AWAY

NOT AT THEIR OWN WILL BUT BY THEIR CHARACTER.

I wasn't asking for perfection. I was asking for attention, for someone to learn me. To know that I wasn't just a surface to touch but a world to explore. I needed someone who could understand that my love language wasn't just about physical gestures but about emotional presence, mutual respect, and the space to be who I truly am.

But they didn't want to learn. They didn't want to know me. They wanted to touch me in ways that suited their own needs, their own desires. They didn't care to understand my essence—only their own distorted image of me.

The Balance They Couldn't See

There's a certain peace that comes from being whole. It's not the kind of peace that others can take from you. Not the kind that's easily broken. It's the kind of peace that radiates from within, the kind that doesn't need anyone else's validation or approval. It's a peace that's so pure and untouched that when someone tries to force themselves into it, they end up burning their own hands.

The men who were interested in me didn't realize this. They were drawn to my peace, my balance, but instead of learning to live in harmony with it, they tried to shake it, to make it fit into their world. They failed to understand that I wasn't here to bend or break for anyone—I was here to stand tall, unshaken, with a foundation so deep that nothing could take me off course.

The Cost of Disrupting the Wholesome

I've watched people destroy themselves trying to tear apart what they didn't understand. They thought they could *change* me, make me into something they could control. They thought my wholeness was an invitation to impose their ideas on me. But what they didn't realize is that my peace wasn't for sale. And when you try to take something from someone who's at peace, you don't just lose them— you lose yourself.

They can touch you, hold you, try to force their way into your life, but if they don't truly understand how you want to be touched, how you need to be loved, their attempts will be futile (unsuccessful). They will break themselves, trying to create chaos in a world that's already perfectly balanced. And in the end, they'll be left with nothing but the empty echoes of what they thought they could control.

The Lesson in Their Loss

I've learned something important from all of this. Something that can't be erased by time or regret. The people who try to disrupt your peace, who fail to understand the depth of your soul, will always be the ones who lose. Because they can never break you. They can only break themselves.

The ones who truly know you don't need to touch you in the wrong ways. They don't need to make you bend or change. They simply need to meet you where you are, to love you for who you already are, not for who they want you to be. And that's a love that **_doesn't disrupt—it flows_**. It elevates.

CHAPTER 08:

I'M DESIRED

Some try to deny it

Yet I enjoy the denial

I don't care for your opinion

Everything looks good with confidence

I walk into a room,

     and I notice eyes looking, heads turning.
Usually, they are intrigued.
I don't need to try. I never do.
It's in the way I stand.
My aura.

     I believe I exude some kind of light,

     an energy that draws people in.
The way my eyes catch the light.
The way my confidence fills every space I enter.
A force I don't ask for, but I welcome.

They look.
They wonder.
But I already know what they're thinking.
It's the look you give a baby,
because you know babies are wholesome and cute.
It's a weird statement,
but it's true.
My energy is just so clean,
outside of how gorgeous I am.

**BABY GIRL YOU ARE
VERY GOOD LOOKING**

I've felt their gaze before,
felt the weight of it,
heavy and hungry,
yet never truly knowing what to do with it.
I've been admired from a distance,
but when it comes time to get close,
the energy shifts.
Because they realize—
they can't possess something this free,
this untouchable.

I DO LOVE CHALLENGE

I LOVE A CONFIDENT SOUL

They look,
but they don't see.
They want,
but they don't understand.
I don't just give myself away.
My energy isn't for everyone,
and the ones who try to take it
without learning how to respect it
will only end up empty-handed.

I am not an object to be desired,
I am a force to be reckoned with.
You can look all you want,
but if you're not worthy of it,
you'll only lose yourself trying to capture me.

I'm not here to be conquered.

I'm here to shine.

And those who are worthy,

will learn that basking in my light

is far more rewarding than trying to control it.

CHAPTER 09:

LOVERS IN DMS

TO WANT ME IS TO WANT TO KNOW ME!

Another message from him.
Another "heart eyes" emoji.
Another man who thinks sending

fire emojis is a personality trait.
They all want me.
But none of them really want *me*.

My DMs are a battlefield,
a parade of men lining up,
dressed in praise, flattery,
all of them swearing they'll treat me like a queen.
But they don't know the rules of the game.
I do.

LET ME TELL YOU WHAT I LIKE

1. HONESTY
2. A MAN THAT IS GOOD FOR HIMSELF
3. SAFETY – EMOTIONALLY, MENTALLY, PHYSICALLY!
4. TO FEEL SOFT AROUND A MAN
5. AN HONORABLE MAN – NOT THE COSPLAY
6. A CREATIVE MIND
7. A MAN WHO APPRECIATES WHAT LIFE HAS TO GIVE
8. THE LITTLE JOY ON HIS FACE WHEN HE DOES SOMETHING HE ENJOYS.
9. A GOOD MAN- GOOD TO ALL NOT JUST SELECTIVE
10. FINALLY, ONE WHO ENJOYS SPORTS BECAUSE I GO CRAZY FOR SOCCER

HONESTY –

When you're honest with yourself,

it's easy to be honest with everyone else.
This is a bare minimum for me.
I'm drawn to the kind of honesty that cuts
through the noise, that doesn't need to be
explained.
I'll follow an honest man until my shoes wear out.
It's magnetic.

A MAN THAT IS GOOD FOR HIMSELF –

Here we are looking for good men. Do we even
know how to identify a good man?
It starts with how he treats himself.
If he sees something being done that doesn't feel
right he objects;
If he's invited to somewhere that doesn't feel
right,
he chooses his peace over pleasing anyone.
That's a man who will choose peace with you, too.

SAFETY – EMOTIONALLY, MENTALLY, PHYSICALLY!

If you don't feel safe with your man—if you feel like your heart, mind, and body are at risk—then he doesn't care for you.
You can tell when someone isn't willing to change, when your safety isn't their priority.
That's when you should run.

SAFETY – a priority!

TO FEEL SOFT AROUND A MAN –

The sweet relief of not having to be
strong all the time.
I want a man who doesn't demand 50/50 but
believes in balance.
Because I'll run from any man who tries to make
me carry the load alone.
But if we're both in this with intention? That's
where the magic happens.

Relationships always work when there're
good intentions of making it work on both ends.
If it's one sided, then yeah its "BAAAAD"

YOU'RE IN THIS
RELATIONSHIP ALONE

AN HONORABLE MAN – NOT THE COSPLAY

There's nothing like knowing a man is good at his core—someone people can vouch for, genuinely.
Not because he puts on a show, but because being good is simply who he is.

MARRY ME PLEASEEEEEEE

Just not kidding. I love being treated with respect, but honestly? A king knows his worth.

A KING

A CREATIVE MIND

As a creative myself, I need someone who gets it.
I need someone who can hold space for my dreams without clouding them.
People who don't understand creativity cause doubts, and I'm not here for that.
I need a mind that thrives alongside mine.

ITS A NO FOR ME IF HE SHAMES ME FOR

THINKING OUTSIDE THE BOX

NOTE; most creatives struggle with doubt.

So this is vague

GRATITUDE

A MAN WHO APPRECIATES WHAT LIFE
HAS TO GIVE

A grateful person will never take you for granted
because they understand how

precious life—and love—really is.
That's the kind of man I want by my side.

A GOOD MAN. GOOD TO ALL NOT JUST
SELECTIVE –

A good person doesn't choose when to be good.
A good person is kind, even when it's not easy.
A good man listens, not just when it benefits him,

		but because he genuinely cares.
That's who I'll always choose.

FINALLY, ONE WHO ENJOYS SPORTS
BECAUSE I GO CRAZY FOR SOCCER

Let's be real, I've tried to compromise.
But nothing beats sharing a soccer moment with
someone—
whether it's a win or a loss, it's pure joy.
It's more than just a sport to me. It's ART.

THE LITTLE JOY ON HIS FACE WHEN HE
DOES SOMETHING HE ENJOYS.

When I see him push his limits in the
gym,
Or when he discovers something new,
Or when he scores that goal—
It's the simple joy that gets me.
Men, when they're truly happy?

That's the kind of adorable I'm talking
about.

Its SOOO cute

To me?

One after another, they claim they're different,
that they're the one who'll show me real love.
But none of them have the patience,
none of them have the depth.
They love bomb,
fill up my DMs like they're throwing candy at a parade.
It's exhausting.

I give them a chance.

One in particular catches my eye—*name redacted for privacy.*
He's wanted me for years,
waiting for the perfect moment to swoop in.
He gets a place for himself, graduates,
and thinks now's the time.
Now's the time for us.
I give him that chance.

But here's where the game changes.
He starts giving me the silent treatment.
Why? Because I went on vacation.
To Senegal. Took a picture with a local.
And just like that, he's convinced I've betrayed him.
What is it about a man's ego that makes a local picture feel like a betrayal?

I'll tell you what.. insecurities

He goes through my phone.
My phone.

Trying to find anything to prove

I'm unfaithful.
The irony?
He finds nothing.
Just a bunch of pictures of me and friends,

some guy friends
living my life.
But he's embarrassed now,
embarrassed because there's

nothing there to confirm his fears.

I laugh,
though it's bitter.
I gave him a chance.
We knew each other for so long,
yet here he is,
silent, upset,
too proud to admit his mistake.
I broke it off.

I told him I couldn't continue this and **blocked him**

He doesn't leave me alone, though.
Messages, calls, pleas.
"Let's work it out."
"Why are you doing this to me?"
But I've seen enough.
He was never ready for me.
He was never ready for anything.

The truth is,
I loved him.
I truly did.
But love can't survive projecting insecurities.
It can't survive projecting jealousy without reason.
It can't survive silence in place of honesty.

I also don't think he's a good person anymore.

He wants people to see him as a
good person

*He's a bad person who is
sometimes good.*

A good person is always good.

Another message pops up.
This time, I don't even open it.
I'm done with love bombs.
Done with the chase.
I'm laughing,
but the laugh is a little sad,
because I know I'm worth more than this.
And I'm tired of giving chances
to men who don't want to see what's right in front of
them.

CHAPTER 10:

UNHINGED (PART TWO)

un·hinged

/ˌənˈhinjd/

———

adjective

1. mentally unbalanced; deranged.

"Unhinged, But Home Again"

Meaning

"Lost Her Mind, Found Her Way"

Chapter 10: Unhinged (The second part).

We lost our minds.

Do not worry, my love. This chapter? A gloat.

A gloat about our sanity, because, trust me,

we're reclaiming it with a fierceness you've never seen.
It's called *unhinged* because we've got our sanity back,

and now—now we reflect.

Let's dive in, my lovers.

The rest of these chapters will give you hope.

Help you understand what it really means
to be a lover girl.

I love you.
All of you.

Ok, NOW—let's dive in.

See, once I find out you are a
horrible person,
You will never, ever find comfort in my
presence.
Do not worry; this isn't dark,
It's your guidance. As a lover girl, you
must, and I mean **must**—withhold
morality.
It is what lights you up.
You will radiate love.
The more you radiate love,
The more you tap into your lover girl.

You walked this journey with me.
My first heartbeat, where love was introduced to me as a
reflection—through words.

I didn't understand it, but I *felt* it.
It was very warm, so I liked it.

Ok… It was good, then it turned bad.
Then the roller coasters.
Which created hurt and pain.
And that pain, my love, was embedded within me.
It went on for so long without me even realizing it.
It reflected in **Caught Me at the Right Time**—Chapter
3.

Love Bombed—Chapter 4.

I was very hurt. I felt tormented and targeted.

Me or Her—Chapter 5. My goodness, was my self-worth on the floor.

See **Chapter 6—Princess Treatment**, I was slowly getting back to myself. But that journey gave me a realization:

I was the problem.

I used the pain properly, though, because I realized how I had been traumatized and conditioned.

I never allowed myself to heal. I accumulated pain after pain after pain.

See, the thing with taking on pain is this:
When you lack realization, you are just a product
of the world.
But when you start addressing the pain, the
patterns, and start fixing them—
You become *part* of the world.

So remember, my lovers:
**YOU WANT TO BE OF THE
WORLD, NOT BE MADE BY THE
WORLD.**

The world will always only

Make you what it wants you to be

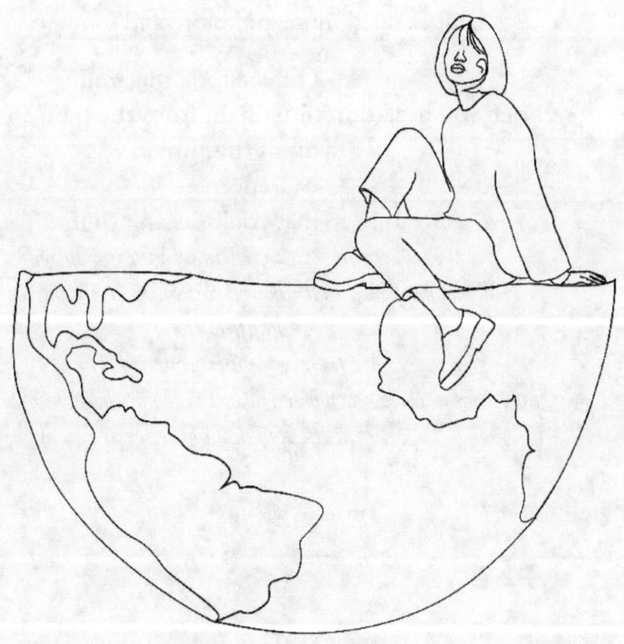

Now, when getting to being "DESIRED," the
healing phase—

immense.
I had been so deep in it, that not only did I pick up my
self-worth from the floor,
But I added more and more and more to it.

I understood this truth:
When you heal, **don't just heal from the pain that hurt
you at the time.**
Go deeper.
Go so deep that you're asking yourself:
What mental state was I in when this occurred?
*What happened that allowed this to happen to me, even
subconsciously?*
Are there any other wounds left?
*Can I heal to the point where I won't flinch at the sight of this thing,
or at the sound of old triggers?*

Alright, I hear you—let's get to the unhinged part.
It's positive, I promise.
Not the wild, crazy unhinged you're thinking of.

This kind of unhinged gave me a realization:
There wasn't any medication that could remove the pain away.
No over-the-counter pills; they were temporary.
This pain was so expensive that it drove me to make decisions subconsciously that added more pain to the pain.

Projections. Insecurities. Wanting to be picked. And it goes on...
What I realized was this: **YOU are your medicine.**

The cure was always within me.
Why? Because it started with innocence.
With innocence came good intentions and
a sense of self.
And so, I just needed to get back there.
But how? How was I going to get there
with all this pain?

Well, baby, I became unhinged.
First, I knew I had to understand what I was going
through.
Then I needed to take a step back.
How do I do this when I love human interactions
and also need to

limit my exposure to anything that would
add new wounds to the existing ones?

I focused on maintaining my self-awareness,
which helped reduce projections.

This allowed me to engage socially
without hurting innocent people who

hadn't contributed to my pain.

Remember when I told you it was a good
kind of unhinged?
I'm getting there.

I came to a realization:
All of this pain I was going through—
There was a source. A *beginning* source.
So I had to go back there.
Not just mentally, but physically.

A therapist would call it confrontation; I
would call it getting rid of my problems.

So here's how I became
unhinged:
I sat with myself and analyzed all the pain.
Where did it come from?
I came up with a strategy. Remember, we
are Humanitarians, lol—

so if these people are out here causing us
pain,

we must make sure they don't
cause anyone else any more pain.
Well, we can try our best.

> I, for one, am a lover girl.
> They seem to forget this.
> There is depth in being a lover girl.
> You want to learn about people so you
> can give them the love they deserve.
> But through that process, you also learn
> about their weaknesses.
> One thing they all have in common: they
> are selfish,
>
> fragile, insecure, and they hide
> their true selves.
>
> Why do they hide their true selves?
> Because they know they are no good,
>
> and people would notice it—and not
> want them around.

So here's what I did, my love, to "Return
the pain to sender":
One by one, I sat with myself, went back to each
pain,

where it originated, and returned it to
them.

Let me give you a visual:
Let's say a family member has been causing

chaos—gaslighting, stealing, lying on my
name.
They are telling me their weaknesses: they are
afraid to be wrong.

To admit they're wrong. It will cause
them immense shame.

Remember; The goal is to make them aware of what they're doing but in a direct way; reflecting to them what they have done and the pain they have caused on to us.

Usually, these kind of people do not like to take accountability,

or admit they are wrong.

This is how I get them to stop:
I keep receipts.
Just as much as they collect flying monkeys,

I start letting people around us know.
It's valid,

because my flying monkeys have experienced the same thing in the

hands of this person—

and this person gaslit them too.
So what you do is you allow this person to think they can do things to you again.

That they can get away with it.
But this time—you are prepared.
I'm not using *prepared* lightly.
You must be prepared to corner them.
The right way.
Expose them right then and there.
They must feel the pain they've been
trying to cause you for all these years.

And that, my love,

is how I gave all of them back the pain
they gave me—that was never mine.

That was the unhinged medicine

I concocted through therapy and my self-work journey.
It's a dangerous method.
You must have your self-esteem in place and—

be ready for this person to play the victim
and turn you into the villain.
Don't try this at home—or on your own. It's
draining.

Well, you see—I was very unhinged.
I had had enough of people, especially the ones I
genuinely loved—and still love.
Because at the end of the day, we are lover girls.
We lead with love.
And so, we must finish with love.

We're ARE good -- baddies

We do bad things for a good reason!

I love you, my lovers.
XOXO
LOVER GIRL X HAWA WHO

CHAPTER 11:

FLEETING BUT REAL

Revenge is never as sweet as they say.

It comes coated in adrenaline, and leaves a bitter aftertaste.

In the moment, it felt right— necessary, even.

They needed to see themselves, and I… I needed them gone.

So, I became their mirror. Every lie they told me,

I reflected. Every wound they caused, I reflected in return.

And it worked..

They couldn't stand the sight of themselves.

The truth chased them
away, just like I knew it would.

But afterward? God, it felt wrong.

Like I'd dipped my clean hands into their mess… and stained myself.

Our hearts are pure— meant to love,

not fight. And yet, love sometimes
demands that we fight for it.

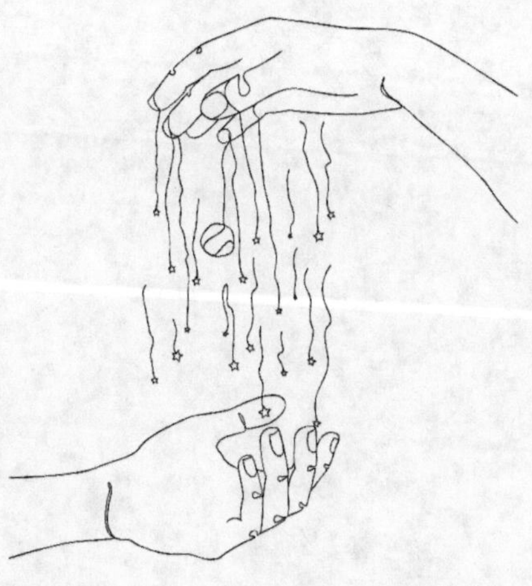

I didn't lose myself, but I didn't feel whole either. Victory left me hollow.

There's a weight that comes with showing people their darkness.

It's fleeting, but it's real.

And maybe they

needed to see it…

but did I need to be the
one to show it? That question
lingers.

Real hearts don't celebrate revenge.

Not really. They carry the ache of knowing it had to be done.

The guilt… the cringe… it's all part of it. But so is the relief of finally being free.

Real to you. Real to me. And
that's enough to let it go.

CHAPTER 12:

LOVERS AND DREAMS

Lovers and dreams,
we met where the impossible is born,
where hearts don't follow time
but pulse to their own rhythm.

In the quiet of
midnight,
we don't need words.
We breathe each other
in,
in a space where dreams
have no limits.

I see you in my dreams,
and I see you in the silence.
You, the one I wasn't meant to find,
but here you are, impossible and true.

Our love is a language
that doesn't need to be spoken,
just felt.
A connection that exists
beyond the waking world.

In dreams, we're endless.
We are what the world cannot define,
flying free through the untold skies
where only the brave dare to chase.

Lovers don't just exist in daylight—
they bloom in the quiet places,
where every touch is a secret,
every kiss a promise
written in the stars.

Lovers are dreamers,
and dreamers are wanderers.
We travel through shadows,
through places where no one else dares to go.

In the space between us,
there's a universe of possibility—
where pain doesn't last,
where love doesn't fade.

      Lovers dream of what could be,
of the spaces where we meet
without fear,
without doubt.

      We paint pictures in the dark,
and live them out in the light,
turning the impossible into the real.

But not every dream is perfect.
Sometimes, the darkness speaks louder.
Sometimes, the shadows whisper things
we can't escape.

Yet, even in the dark,
our love is a spark,
flickering,
but never gone.

When I dream of you,
I dream of the way your soul touches
mine.
It's never just about the touch of skin—
it's the touch of two worlds coming alive.

       Lovers and dreams—they're the
same.
One builds you up,
and the other holds you tight
when you're about to break.

We are dreamers,
we are lovers,
we are the ones who turn every "maybe"
into a resounding "yes."

And when the world
tries to tear us apart,
we hold on tighter,
knowing that the dreams we
chase
are stronger than any fear.

So love me in your dreams,
and I'll love you in mine.
When the morning comes,
we'll be just as we were—
lovers, still,
dreamers, always.

       In our hearts,
we know—
love and dreams never die,
they just keep coming back.

CHAPTER 13:

YOU'RE A LOVER GIRL

un·der·stand /ˌəndərˈstand/

verb

1. To know or grasp the meaning, significance, or nature of something.

2. To accept, acknowledge, and embrace your truth.

You're a Lover Girl.

It's not a title, babe. It's a way of living. It's a philosophy.

For so long, you thought being a lover girl meant falling for the wrong people, giving too much, loving too hard, and hoping that someone would see you the way you deserve to be seen.

But baby girl, that's not it. Not even close.

Being a lover girl is about *you*—about loving yourself with the intensity that you once reserved for everyone else. It's about becoming so full of love, so aligned with who you are, that you radiate a light others can't help but be drawn to.

THE SHIFT

We've walked this journey, haven't we?

The heartbreaks, the mistakes, the lessons we learned the hard way. We've all been there. Loving with reckless abandon, thinking that's what it meant to be a lover girl.

But now? Oh, now you're different.

This chapter isn't about those old patterns. No more seeking love in places that didn't know how to give it back. No more waiting for validation, or for someone else to give you permission to be your full, beautiful self.

This chapter is about growth. Healing. And the radical shift that happens when you start to *love yourself* as fiercely as you loved others.

So let's take a breath and reflect.

REFLECTION AND RELEASE

In the past, you may have given your heart to people who didn't appreciate it. But here's the thing: **you were never the problem**. They were.

You loved. And that was *your* truth. It wasn't wrong. You weren't wrong. The people who couldn't recognize that? That's on them, not you.

And once you realized that—once you understood that love isn't about being with someone who doesn't know how to handle your heart—you became free.

Free to love yourself. Free to let go of the past, the hurt, and the negative thoughts that tried to hold you back. Free to step into your power as a lover girl who knows exactly what she wants and, more importantly, what she deserves.

YOU'RE A LOVER GIRL BECAUSE YOU KNOW YOUR WORTH

Listen, I want you to understand this: **You are worth everything you desire.**

That's it. Full stop.

The love you give to others should never come at the cost of losing yourself. The love you give should always be reciprocal. And when it isn't, you walk away, *and you do it with your head held high.*

There's no shame in walking away from what doesn't serve you. In fact, it's the bravest thing you can do.

But here's the kicker: when you step into your power, you *stop needing validation.* You stop searching for love in places where it doesn't exist. You stop doubting your worth because, honey, you know you're worthy.

Being a lover girl means you've reached a place where you no longer chase love—you *attract* it. Because you know your value, and when you know your worth, others can't help but see it, too.

EMBRACE THE HEALING

Let's talk healing, darling.

Healing doesn't mean you're "fixed." It means you've gotten to a point where you've seen your scars and said, *I'm still beautiful.*

Healing means accepting that you've been through a lot— but you've made it through. And that's a big deal.

You're not defined by your past. Your scars don't make you ugly. They make you resilient. They make you real. They make you *strong*.

Now, healing isn't a straight line. There's no quick fix or magic pill. It's messy. It's beautiful. It's ugly. But it's worth it.

When you heal, you gain clarity. You gain self-love. And you start to see the world differently. You begin to recognize the red flags, set your boundaries, and walk away from what no longer aligns with your purpose.

And here's the thing: the more you heal, the more your heart expands. The more love you have to give to others— and to yourself.

THE NEW YOU

Remember when you didn't think you could make it out of the darkness?

When you didn't think you'd ever be whole again? Well, look at you now.

You're standing in your power. You're a lover girl, unapologetically.

You've learned how to take all the love you once gave away and pour it into yourself.

And let me tell you—*you are glowing*.

This isn't about arrogance. It's about knowing your value. It's about understanding that you're deserving of all the love, success,

and happiness that the world has to offer. You've walked through the fire, babe, and come out stronger.

And now, you're ready to radiate.

LOVING FROM A PLACE OF ABUNDANCE

When you love yourself, everything changes.

You no longer give love from a place of scarcity. You give love from a place of *abundance*.

You're not looking for someone to complete you—you're already complete.

You don't settle anymore. You don't chase after love; you let it come to you.

And when it does, you don't give it all away at once. You cherish it.

You nurture it. But most importantly, you *protect it*.

You protect your heart and energy like the precious gifts they are.

You give love, but you don't lose yourself in it.

You give, and you receive, but you never give more than what you can handle.

THE LOVE YOU DESERVE

So, what does love look like now?

It looks like boundaries. It looks like deep self-respect.

It looks like trust in your own intuition.

It looks like walking away when you need to, and standing tall

when it's time to fight for what's yours.

It looks like being surrounded by people who *see you*,

who celebrate you, and who value you for the amazing person that you are.

It looks like saying "no" without guilt, saying "yes" when it aligns with your soul,

and knowing that your peace of mind is sacred.

Love, real love, starts with you. And once you master that,

it flows effortlessly into every area of your life.

LETTING GO OF THE OLD

Now, let's talk about releasing what no longer serves you.

This is a powerful part of becoming a lover girl—

letting go of the things that kept you stuck.

Whether it's old beliefs, past relationships,

or toxic people—let them go.

It's time to release the weight.

Drop the baggage. Clear the space in your heart and life for what truly belongs there.

You deserve to have a life filled with joy, peace, and authentic connections.

So make room for them.

LOVE WITH NO CONDITIONS

This is what I want you to know:

You don't have to prove anything.

You don't have to be anyone's savior.

You don't have to change who you are to fit into someone else's narrative.

You are enough, exactly as you are.

And the love you give is a reflection of that truth.

It's powerful. It's transformative. And it's boundless.

But it starts with you. Always.

You're a lover girl because you know how to love without conditions.

You love yourself, you love others, and you love life with a fierce and unapologetic heart.

Catching Love, Letting Go

The love you seek is not something you have to chase endlessly.

Instead, it's something that finds its way to you when you stop clinging to the past,

to the things that don't serve you anymore.

By catching love within yourself, by learning how to let go of attachments,

you create space for the love that's meant for you. It's a love that's free, unforced, and ever-present.

Letting go doesn't mean losing. It means opening yourself up to the freedom

of love in its purest form. You don't have to hold tight to love.

It will come to you when you least expect it, and when it does, you'll be ready—open and free.

I love you.
All of you.

XOXO MY LOVERS THE GUYZERS AND THE GIRLIES